# Franz Schubert
# FOUR SYMPHONIES
## in Full Score

# Franz Schubert
# FOUR SYMPHONIES
## in Full Score

Symphony No. 4 ("Tragic") in C Minor

Symphony No. 5 in B-flat Major

Symphony No. 8 ("Unfinished") in B Minor

Symphony No. 9 ("Great") in C Major

Edited by
Johannes Brahms

From the Breitkopf & Härtel Complete Works Edition

Dover Publications, Inc., New York

Published in Canada by General Publishing Company, Ltd.,
30 Lesmill Road, Don Mills, Toronto, Ontario.
Published in the United Kingdom by Constable and
Company, Ltd., 10 Orange Street, London WC2H 7EG.

This Dover edition, first published in 1978, is an unabridged
republication of selected sections (Symphonies 4, 5, 8 and
9) from *Serie 1. Symphonien für Orchester* of *Franz
Schubert's Werke. Kritisch durchgesehene Gesammtaus-
gabe*, originally published by Breitkopf & Härtel, Leipzig,
in two volumes, 1884 and 1885.

*International Standard Book Number: 0-486-23681-1*
*Library of Congress Catalog Card Number: 78-54970*

Manufactured in the United States of America
Dover Publications, Inc.
180 Varick Street
New York, N.Y. 10014

# CONTENTS

The D. numbers are those of the entries in the standard reference *Schubert; Thematic Catalogue of All His Works in Chronological Order*, by Otto Erich Deutsch in collaboration with Donald R. Wakeling, published by W. W. Norton & Company Inc., New York, in 1951.

* The nine bars of the unfinished third movement are not included in the present volume.

# Symphony No. 4 ("Tragic") in C Minor

**Allegro vivace.**

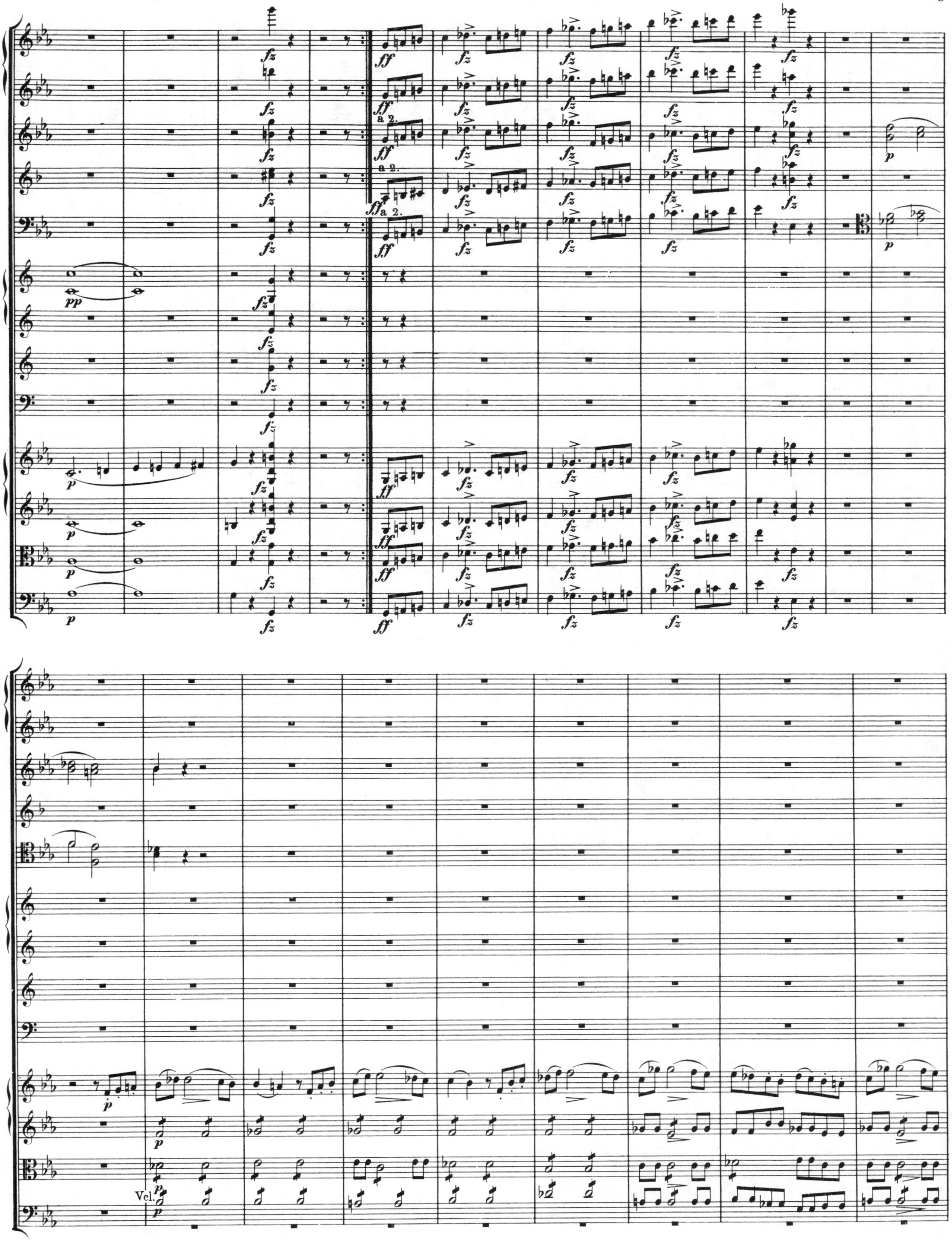
a 2.
a 2.
a 2.
Vcl.

10

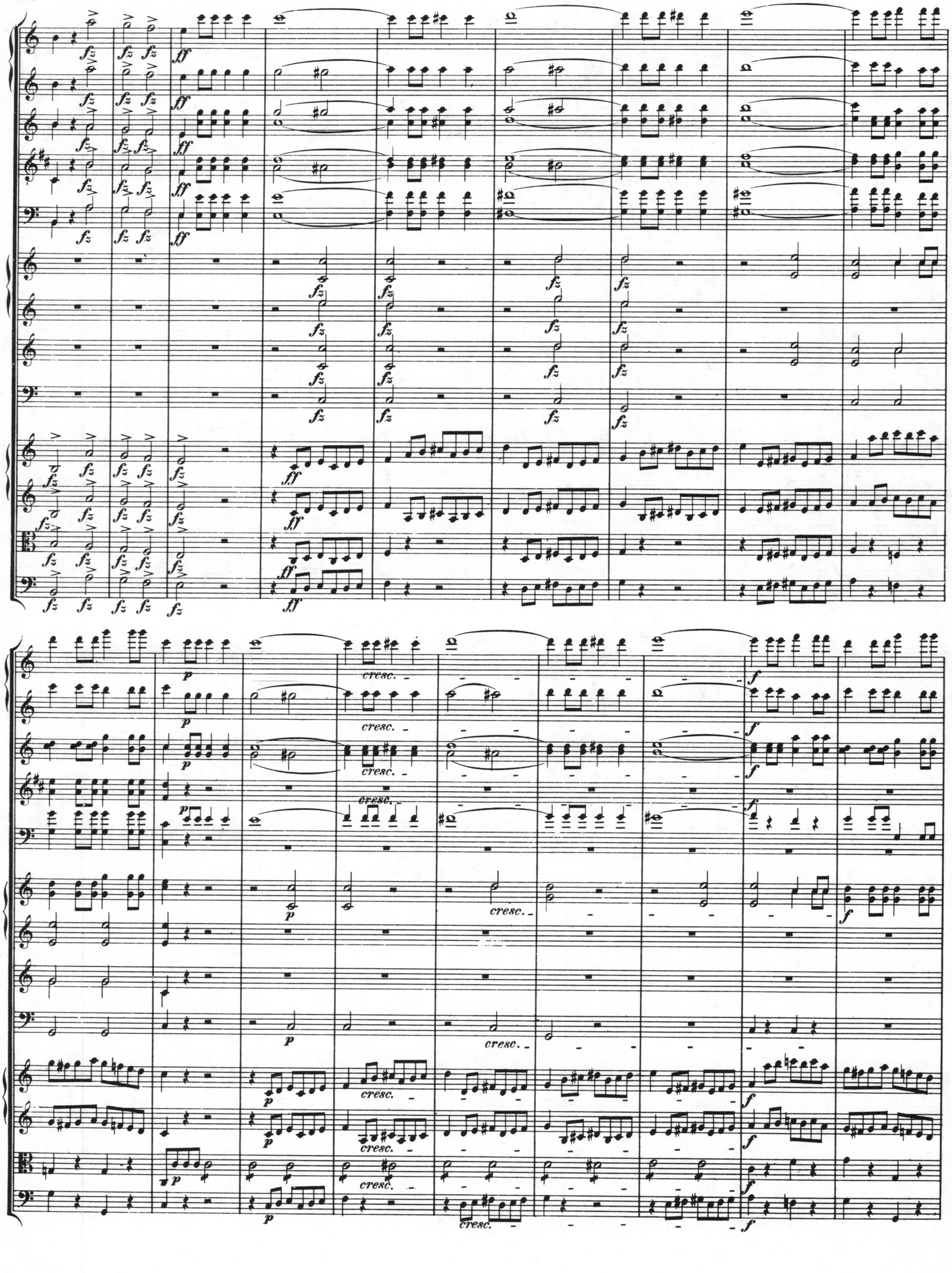
fz
ff
p
cresc.
f

18

**Allegro vivace**

Flauto I.

Flauto II.

Oboi.

Clarinetti in B.

Fagotti.

Corni in Es.

Trombe in Es.

Timpani in Es u. B.

Violino I.

Violino II.

Viola.

Violoncello e Basso.

Men. D. C.

**Allegro.**

Flauto I.

Flauto II.

Oboi.

Clarinetti in B.

Fagotti.

Corni in C.

Corni in Es.

Trombe in C.

Timpani in C.G.

Violino I.

Violino II.

Viola.

Violoncello e Basso.

# Symphony No. 5 in B-flat Major

76

Andante con moto.

Flauto.

Oboi.

Fagotti.

Corni in Es.

Violino I.

Violino II.

Viola.

Violoncello
e Basso.

83

## Menuetto.

### Allegro molto.

Flauto.

Oboi.

Fagotti.

Corni in G.

Violino I.

Violino II.

Viola.

Violoncello e Basso.

TRIO.

Men. D. C.

**Allegro vivace.**

Flauto.

Oboi.

Fagotti.

Corni in B.

Violino I.

Violino II.

Viola.

Violoncello
e Basso.

# Symphony No. 8 ("Unfinished") in B Minor

118

p
p
cresc.
p
cresc.
p
cresc.
p
cresc.
p
ff
ff
ff
ff
ff
ff
cresc.
cresc.
ff
cresc.
ff
cresc.
ff
cresc.
ff
fz
fz
fz
a 2.
fz
fp
pp
a 2.
fz
fp
pp
fz
pp
pp
ff
fz
ff
fz
fz
fz
fz
fz
fz
pp
pizz.
pp
fz

**Andante con moto.**

Flauti.

Oboi.

Clarinetti in A.

Fagotti.

Corni in E.

Trombe in E.

Tromboni. { Alto. Tenore.  Basso.

Timpani in E. H.

Violino I.

Violino II.

Viola.

Violoncello.

Basso.

129

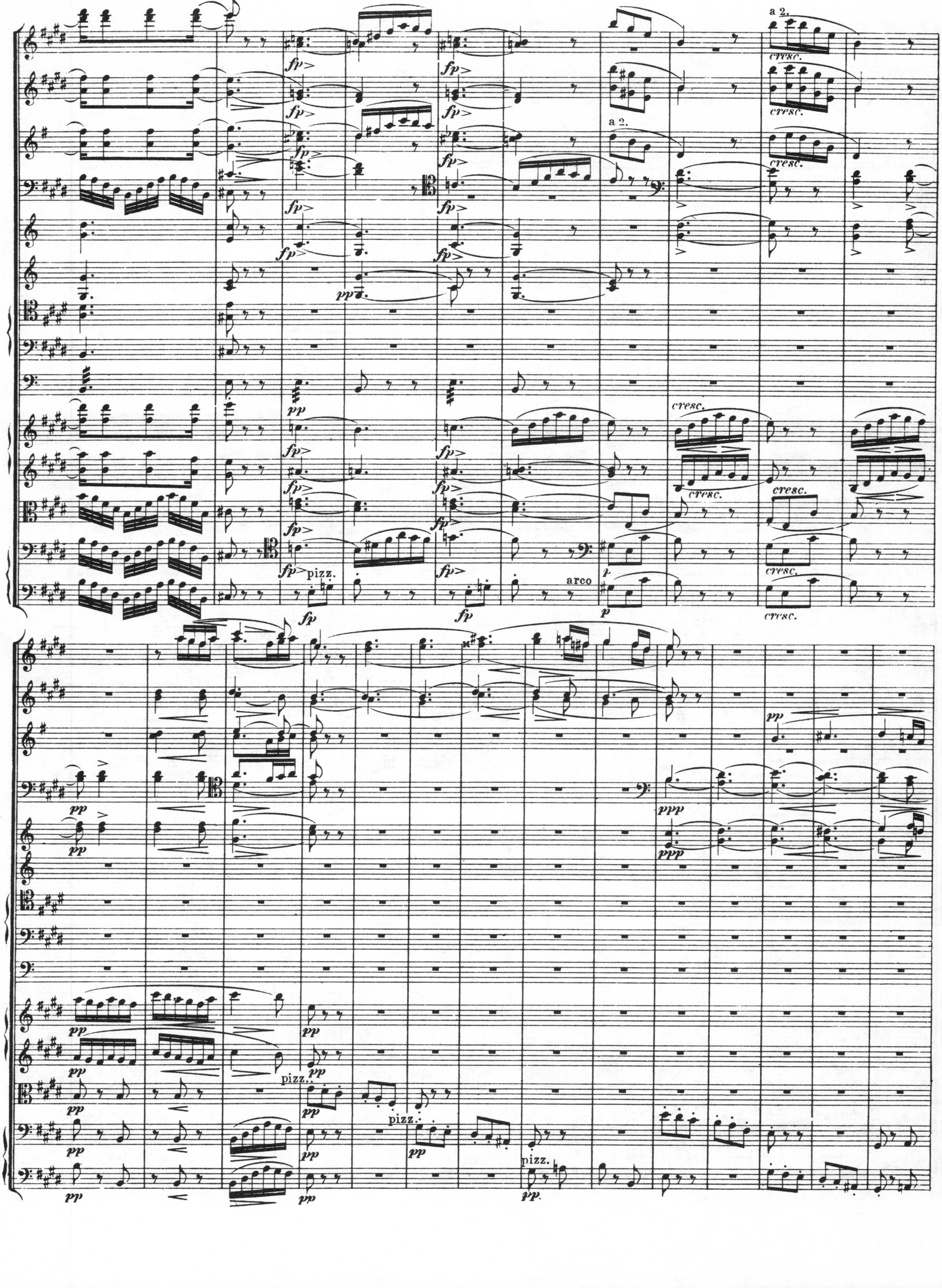
a 2.
cresc.
fp
pp
pizz.
arco
p
ppp

# Symphony No. 9 ("Great") in C Major

**Allegro, ma non troppo.**

156

174

Più moto.

**Andante con moto.**

189

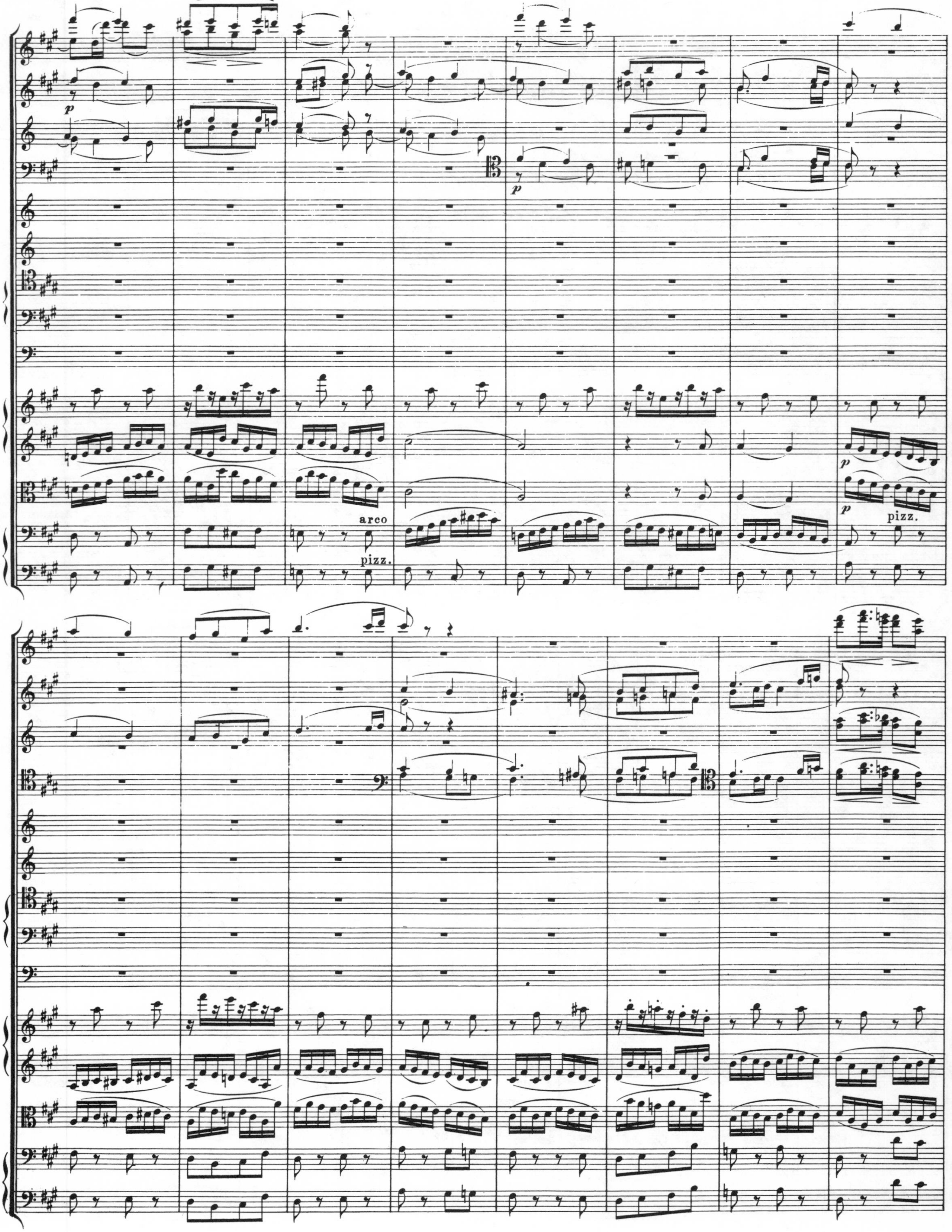
p
arco
pizz.
pizz.

198

Scherzo.
Allegro vivace.

Flauti.

Oboi.

Clarinetti in C.

Fagotti.

Corni in C.

Trombe in C.

Tromboni. {Alto. Tenore. Basso.}

Timpani in C. G.

Violino I.

Violino II.

Viola.

Violoncello.

Basso.

203

204

208

TRIO.

214

Scherzo D. C.

Allegro vivace.

Flauti.

Oboi.

Clarinetti in C.

Fagotti.

Corni in C.

Trombe in C.

Tromboni. Alto. Tenore. Basso.

Timpani in C.G.

Violino I.

Violino II.

Viola.

Violoncello.

Basso.

222

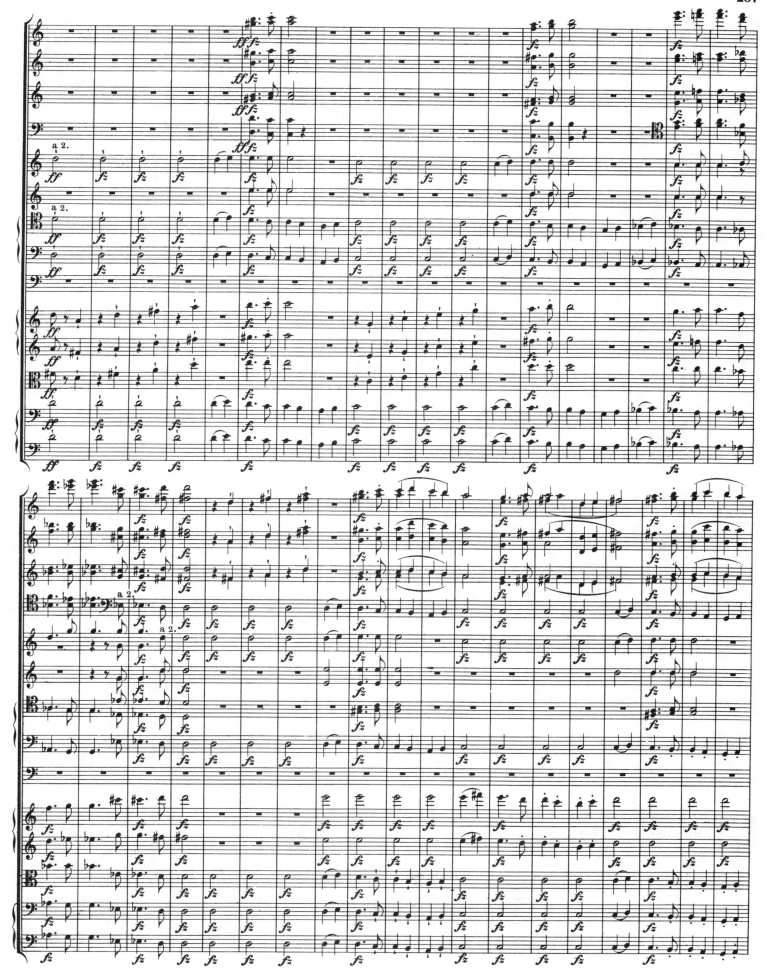

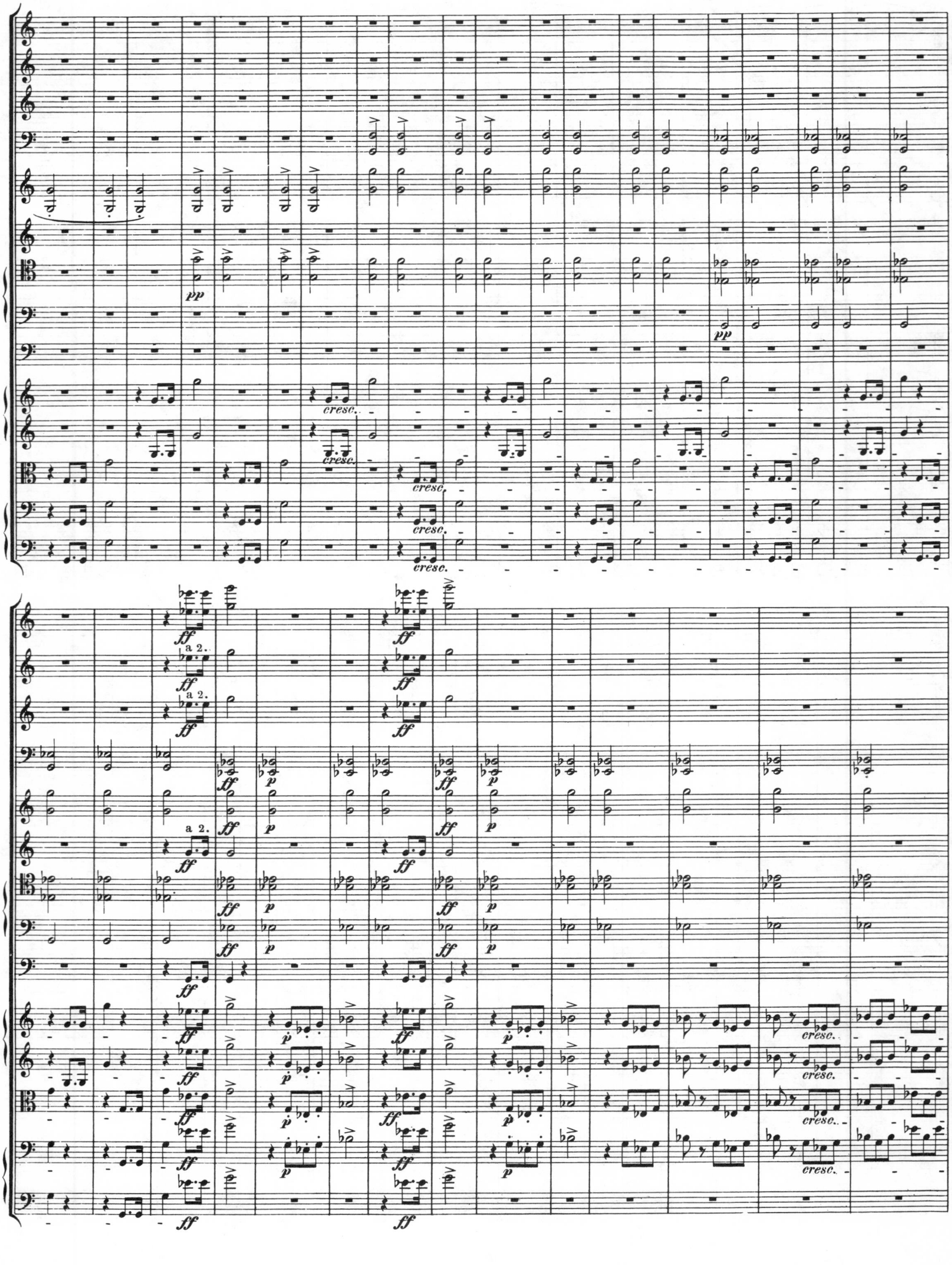
pp
cresc.
a 2.
ff
p